HOW TO DO
GOOD TO MANY

THE PUBLIC GOOD IS THE CHRISTIAN'S LIFE

RICHARD BAXTER

HOW TO DO
GOOD TO MANY

THE PUBLIC GOOD IS THE CHRISTIAN'S LIFE

Edited and with an introduction
by Jordan J. Ballor

GRAND RAPIDS · MICHIGAN

How to Do Good to Many: The Public Good Is the Christian's Life

© 2018 by Jordan J. Ballor

ISBN 978-0-934874-08-3 (paperback)
ISBN 978-0-934874-09-0 (ebook)

CHRISTIAN'S LIBRARY PRESS
*An imprint of the Acton Institute
for the Study of Religion & Liberty*
98 E. Fulton
Grand Rapids, Michigan 49503
616.454.3080
www.clpress.com

Interior composition: Judy Schafer
Cover: Scaturro Design

Printed in the United States of America

CONTENTS

INTRODUCTION

Richard Baxter (1615–1691) was perhaps the most pro-
lific author in the English language during the seventeenth century. He was renowned for his piety, convic-
tion, and erudition, despite his lack of significant formal
education. He was a brilliant autodidact, however, reading widely and variously across traditions and disci-
plines. Baxter's influence in his own time was such that
his magisterial treatment of the relationship between
Protestantism and economic ethics was formative for
the later German sociologist and economic historian
Max Weber (1864–1920), who highlighted Baxter as
the exemplar of the "Protestant ethic."

Baxter was indeed a champion of the legacy of the
Protestant Reformation, and he engaged in significant
controversy over doctrinal matters with Roman Catholics
as well as with more radical figures and those whose
views would corrupt Christianity in England. Because
Baxter's polemic was often pointed, he was famed as a
controversialist, but he nevertheless was clear about

the implications of detailed doctrinal controversies. He understood such disputes to be important but also largely limited to the discourse of learned theologians. So even while he engaged in fierce debates about many of the finer points of Christian doctrine, he likewise articulated a vibrant and vigorous understanding of "mere Christianity," a phrase that appears in this text and was later taken up more famously by the great twentieth-century Christian apologist and scholar C. S. Lewis (1898–1963).

Biographical Sketch

A statue of Richard Baxter erected in Kidderminster, England, in 1875 includes an inscription that describes Baxter as "renowned equally for his Christian learning and his pastoral fidelity." Baxter's ministry in Kidderminster from 1641 to 1660 was especially formative for him and made such an impression that both "churchmen and nonconformists" would work together hundreds of years later to erect the statue in his honor.

Baxter's time in Kidderminster was interrupted by the outbreak of the English Civil War from 1642 through 1646, during which Baxter served as a chaplain for some of Oliver Cromwell's forces. His experience of the lawlessness and comportment of many of the soldiers affected Baxter deeply, and his first publication in 1649, *Aphorisms of Justification*, addressed the relationship between faith and works, the oft-controverted question arising out of the Reformation. Baxter intended to refute antinomianism, the view that the Christian life was not bound by the dictates of the law, but his work was judged by many to have gone too far to the other side. Baxter would later define and refine his own views at great length, often within the context of debates over justification and sanctification. Nevertheless, he would continue to be accused of neonomianism (the improper application of a "new law" on the life of the believer) throughout his career and down to the present.

His views were often idiosyncratic or at least formed over against those that Baxter thought were unduly onerous or affirmed too strongly. He held, for example, to a form of hypothetical universalism and in this way stands in an English theological tradition going back to Bishop John Davenant (1572–1641). Davenant was a member of the English delegation at the international Synod of Dordt (1618–1619), and Baxter would later affirm his agreement with the doctrinal positions arising out of this major ecclesiastical gathering.

In 1660 Charles II ascended the throne of England as well as Scotland and Ireland in the restoration of the monarchy, and Baxter came to London, in part to advocate for a reformed and renewed national church. He had been a nonconformist since before his appointment to Kidderminster by the bishop of Worcester, which had been made in the midst of openness to pastoral reform. He was married in 1662 to the much younger Margaret Charlton, and this latter period of his life was marked by strife, suffering, and struggle even amid his otherwise happy marriage. His preaching and publishing were a constant source of controversy and even legal action, including dispossession, imprisonment, and revocation of rights to preach or teach in public.

Baxter's wife died in 1681, the year before the publication of the present text, *How to Do Good to Many*. As the title page of the publication indicates, the text takes the basic form of a sermon. Despite his sufferings, Baxter was a faithful and diligent servant of God, working as he might to produce occasional treatises, counsels, polemics, and major systematic works as well as sermons and devotions, reflections, and a massive autobiographical text, the *Reliquiae Baxterianae*, published posthumously in 1696. Many of Baxter's works are considered to be classics and are still widely read today, including *The Saints' Everlasting Rest* (1651), *The Reformed Pastor* (1656), and a magisterial four-volume collection of practical theology, *A Christian Directory* (1675).

Major Themes

The two phenomena highlighted in Baxter's Kidderminster statue, "Christian learning" and "pastoral fidelity," capture the emphases not only of his time in the pastorate there but of his entire career. For Baxter the two go together. Truth and goodness are necessarily connected, and Baxter worked tirelessly to explicate and develop their depths and the relationship between them.

Baxter's concern for Christian learning involved efforts to articulate, defend, and clarify Christian doctrine as well as to demonstrate the need for sustained educational efforts in the church and society. His work involved not only exploring Christian doctrine but engaging natural philosophy and early-modern science, atheism as well as heretical and heterodox movements. His most significant works, as he understood them, were his extensive treatments of Christian theology, including his *Catholick Theology* (1675) and especially his only major Latin work, *Methodus Theologiae Christianae* (1681). The *Methodus* was meant to be Baxter's magnum opus, but the reception of Baxter's work was to take a different path.

It was, in fact, Baxter's practical theology and piety which were to exercise the greatest influence on later readers. This is in part because of the appreciation of this aspect of Baxter's work shown by later figures like John Wesley (1703–1791). Baxter's works, particularly those devoted to practical theology, were printed and reprinted in various collections for centuries following his death. A major nineteenth-century effort undertaken by the Scottish Congregationalist minister William Orme (1787–1830) resulted in the publication of *The Practical Works of Richard Baxter*, a twenty-three-volume collection of Baxter's practical treatises, pastoral theology, sermons, and devotions. The series put together over thirteen thousand pages of Baxter's writings, and the present text, *How to Do Good to Many*, appears in the seventeenth volume as part of a series of sermons.

As noted previously, the question of the role of the law in the Christian life was a recurring concern for Baxter. If good conduct must be rooted in truth, so too was proper understanding of the moral requirements of the Christian life necessary for the pursuit of holiness. Many of Baxter's efforts toward pastoral fidelity were manifested in the publication of rigorous and nuanced works of moral and practical theology. He wrote treatises about the proper modes of pastoral oversight and discipline, social order and political authority, the disposition of wealth and stewardship, and the need for and method of education. He provided advice for those in various stations of life, including the married, the young, and the spiritually desolate. For Baxter, the principles of right conduct had to be identified and applied prudently in each particular case. Baxter's wisdom and diligence place him, along with William Perkins (1558–1602) and William Ames (1576–1633), among the greatest of the English-language casuists, or theologians rendering guidance through so-called cases of conscience. His major work of casuistry is *A Christian Directory*, which examines personal ethics as well as ethical principles and problems in the major social institutions: family, church, and government.

Significance of This Text

How to Do Good to Many: Or, the Public Good Is the Christian's Life, stands as a prime exemplar of Baxter's twin concerns for doctrinal as well as practical fidelity. Baxter's point of departure is Galatians 6:10, in which the apostle Paul exhorts his hearers, "As we have opportunity, let us do good to all, especially to those who are of the household of faith." Both Baxter's erudition and his wisdom are on display in this treatise.

He opens in a kind of scholastic fashion, first determining the scope of his treatment and defining the terms before proceeding to more detailed discussions about how to do good in the world. A few features of Baxter's treatment are worthy of particular attention.

Baxter roots his discussion of the ethical demands of human life in both nature and special revelation. The text is an extended sermon on Galatians 6:10, but Baxter also works logically out of fundamental principles of human nature and society. The doctrine Baxter explicates is that "to do good to all is all men's duty." It is a moral requirement of human nature to do good to others. Furthermore, contends Baxter, because of his regeneration and calling to serve Christ, "every Christian especially must apply himself" to this good work.

This understanding of created nature and saving grace undergirds Baxter's discussion and comes to the fore explicitly in his discussion of the relationship and relative value of temporal and eternal or spiritual goods. In this way Baxter distinguishes between an order of ultimate value, or what he calls "the order of estimation," and an order of proximity or time, or what he calls the "order of execution." He advises his audience, for example, to "do as much good as you are able to men's bodies in order to the greater good of souls." He supports this directive by arguing that "if nature be not supported, men are not capable of other good." By this he means that "we pray for our daily bread before pardon and spiritual blessings, not as if it were better, but that nature is supposed before grace," and, significantly, "we cannot be Christians if we are not men."

This perspective on nature and grace also manifests in Baxter's understanding of the proper use of temporal goods and wealth. They are to be appreciated in themselves as God's good gifts but must also be properly oriented toward greater goods. This goes for the individual's concerns in both this world and the next. In this world, each person is called to enlarge his or her perspective to embrace more than just individual good. In connection with this, Baxter articulates a version of subsidiarity, a classical Christian doctrine emphasizing the moral significance of proximity. "But as all motion and action is first upon the nearest object," writes Baxter, "so must ours, and doing good must be in order. First, we must begin at home with our own souls and lives, and next to our nearest relations, friends, acquaintances, and neighbors, and then to our societies, church and kingdom, and all the world."

And the goods of this world are to be employed in light of the weight of eternity. Thus, writes Baxter, "every man has his estate from God, and for God, and is bound as his steward accordingly to use it." Throughout the treatise Baxter explores various examples of those who improperly value temporal goods over spiritual goods or who construe their own earthly wealth as fit to be used for luxury, idleness, or sin. Baxter is thus particularly critical of those who would value the earthly toil of slaves more than the eternal destiny of their souls. He engages the social as well as spiritual problems of slavery, condemning it while realizing the complex challenges it represents. With respect to laws that would set converted slaves free, for instance, Baxter reproves the resistance of slave owners to allow for the evangelization of their slaves. "Is it not an odious crime for Christians to hinder the conversion of these infidels, lest they lose their service by it, and to prefer their gain before men's souls?" he asks.

If Baxter stands as a preeminent representative of the Protestant ethic, then this treatise is a salient summary statement of his ethical approach and conclusions. His earnest call for Christians to do good to many and his explorations of prudent stewardship, which apply to all Christians of whatever station, is a classic statement of Protestant social thought and one that continues to have wisdom today.

Editorial Notes

The present text has been updated into contemporary English. In some cases obsolete or archaic words have been replaced with more common contemporary words. The punctuation has been modernized and made more consistent. Section headings have been added and a more consistent subsection outline has been imposed here, with the goal of clarifying the overall organization of the treatise. In some cases this edition follows the judgments made by Orme, but overall the changes to this edition are much more significant than the changes to earlier versions. Where Baxter clearly alludes to or quotes Scripture without attribution, a reference has been added in brackets. Baxter's original text uses the

King James Version of Scripture, and to make the text more readable and consistent these references have been updated to the New King James Version where doing so would not introduce confusion. The few footnotes that are present have been added and are intended to clarify some of the references Baxter makes or to make explicit some terminology that might otherwise not be common for contemporary audiences. In some cases the word order has been updated to read more smoothly, although this necessarily involves some subjective judgments. The text in this published edition has been put together with the goal of facilitating reading by a contemporary audience. The seventeenth-century publication as well as the nineteenth-century edition by Orme are both readily available digitally for those who would rather read earlier versions of Baxter's classic text.

—Jordan J. Ballor
Acton Institute

How to do Good to Many:

OR, THE

PUBLICK GOOD

IS THE

Chriſtians Life.

DIRECTIONS and MOTIVES to it.

Intended for an AUDITORY of

London Citizens,

AND

Publiſhed for them, for want of leave to preach them.

By *RICHARD BAXTER.*

Tit. 2. 14. *Who gave himſelf for us, that he might redeem us from all iniquity, and purifie to himſelf a People zealous of good Works.*

LONDON,
Printed for *Rob. Gibs* at the Ball in *Chancery Lane,* 1682.

To the Truly Christian Merchants and Other Citizens of London

As my disease and the restraint of rulers seem to tell me that my pulpit work is at an end, so also my abode among you, or in this world, cannot be long. What work I have lived for I have given the world more durable notice than transient words. It has been such as men in power were against and, it seems, will no longer endure. What doctrine it was that I last prepared for you I thought meet to desire the press thus to tell you, not to vindicate myself nor to characterize them who think that it deserves six months' imprisonment, but to be in your hands a provocation and direction for that great work of a Christian life, which sincerely done will prepare you for that safety, joy, and glory that London, England, or earth will not afford and men or devils cannot take from you. When through the meritorious righteousness of Christ your holy love and good works to him in his brethren shall make you the joyful objects of that sentence, "Come, you blessed of My Father, inherit the kingdom" [Matt. 25:34], this is the life that need not be repented of as spent in vain.

Dear friends, in this farewell I return you my most hearty thanks for your extraordinary love and kindness to myself, and much more for your love to Christ and to his servants, who have more needed your relief. God is not unjust; he will not forget your work and labor of love. You have visited those whom others imprisoned and fed those whom others brought into want, and when some ceased not to preach for our affliction, it quenched not your impartial charity. It has been an unspeakable mercy unto me almost all my days (when I received nothing from them) to have known so great a number as I have done of serious, humble, holy, charitable Christians, in whom I saw that Christ has an elect, peculiar people, quite different from the brutish, proud, hypocritical, malignant, unbelieving world! O how sweet has the familiarity of such been to me, whom the ignorant world has hated! Most of them are gone to Christ; I am following. We leave you here to longer trial. It is likely you have a bitter cup to drink. But be faithful to the death, and Christ will give you the Crown of Life. The word of God is not bound, and the Jerusalem above is free [Gal. 4:26], where is the general assembly of the firstborn, an innumerable company of angels, the spirits of the just made perfect, with Christ their glorified Head. The Lord guide, bless, and preserve you.

PREFACE

*As we have opportunity, let us do good
to all, especially to those who are of the
household of faith.*
—Galatians 6:10

Good is an epithet of the highest signification of any in
human language. Some think the name God is thence
derived. Greatness and wisdom are equally his attributes, but goodness is the completion and sweetest to
the creature. Christ appropriates it to God to be good—
that is, essentially, primarily, and perfectly, as well as
universally communicative [Matt. 19:17]. When it is
said that God is love [1 John 4:8], the sense is the same,
that he is the infinite, essential, efficiently, and finally
amiable, perfect good.

But though no one of his attributes in propriety and
perfection is communicable (else he that has one part of
the Deity must have all), yet he imprints his similitude
and image on his works. And the impress of his love and

goodness is the chief part of his image on his saints. This is their very holiness. For this is the chief part of their likeness to God and dedication to him. When the Spirit of sanctification is described in Scripture as given upon believing, it signifies that our faithful perception of the redeeming, saving love of God in Christ is that means which the Spirit of Christ will bless to the operating of the habit of holy love to God and man. This becomes a new and divine nature to the soul, and is sanctification itself, and the true principle of a holy, evangelical conversion. And as it is said of God that he is good and does good, so everything is inclined to work as it is. Christ tells us the good tree will bring forth good fruits [Matt. 7:17], and so on. And we are God's "workmanship, created in Christ Jesus for good works, which God prepared beforehand that we should walk in them" (Eph. 2:10).

Yet man does good not as the sun shines, that is, by a full bent of natural necessitation, or else the world would not be as it is. But man acts as a free, undetermined agent who has need to be commanded by a law and stirred up by manifold motives and exhortations such as the Holy Ghost here uses in the text.

Where:

1. *Doing good* is the substance of the duty.

2. *Men* are the objects.

3. To *all men* is the extent.

4. Especially to them of *the household of faith* is the direction for precedence.

5. And *while we have opportunity* is the season, including a motive to make haste.

So large and excellent a theme would require more than my allotted time to handle it fully. Therefore I shall now confine myself to the duty extended: "Do good to all men."

Doctrine: *To do good to all men is all men's duty, to which every Christian especially must apply himself.*

All men *should* do it: true Christians *can* do it, through grace, and *must* do it, and *will* do it. A good man is a common good. Christ's Spirit in them is not a dead or idle principle. It makes them in their several measures the salt of the earth and the lights of the world. They are fruitful branches in the true vine. Every grace tends to well-doing and to the good of the whole body, for which each single member is made. Even hypocrites, as wooden legs, are serviceable to the body, but every living member much more, except some diseased ones, who may be more troublesome and dangerous than the wooden leg. It is a sign he is a branch cut off and withered who cares little for any but himself.

The malignant disciple of the devil hates the true and spiritual good. The ignorant do not know good from evil. The erroneous take evil for good and falsehood for truth. The slothful hypocrite wishes much good but does little. The formal ceremonious hypocrite extols the name and image of goodness. The worldly hypocrite will do good if he can do it cheaply, without any loss or suffering to his flesh. The libertine hypocrite pleads Christ's merits against the necessity of doing good and looks to be saved because Christ is good, though he himself is barren and ungodly; and some ignorant teachers have taught them to say, when they can find no true faith, repentance, holiness, or obedience in themselves, that it is enough to believe that Christ believed and repented for them and was holy and obedient for them. He was indeed holy and obedient for penitent believers, not to make holiness and obedience unnecessary to them, but to make them sincerely holy and obedient to himself and to excuse them from the necessity of that perfect holiness and obedience here, which is necessary to those who will be justified by the law of works or innocence. Thus all sorts of bad men have their oppositions to doing good. But to the sincere Christian it is made as natural. His heart is set upon it. He is created and redeemed and sanctified for it, as the tree is made for fruit. He studies it as the chief trade and business that he lives for. He wakes for it. Yes, he sleeps and eats and drinks for it, even to enable his body to serve his soul in serving that Lord whose redeemed peculiar people are all "zealous for good works" (Titus 2:14). The measure of this zeal of doing good is the utmost of their power, with all their talents, in desire and sincere endeavor. The extent of the object is to all (though not to all alike)—that is, to as many as they can.

But for order's sake we must here consider:

1. Who this all means, and in what order

2. What is *good*, and what is that good which we must do

3. What rules he must observe in doing it

4. What qualifications he must have that will do good to many

5. What works must be done by him who would do good to many

6. What motives should quicken us to the practice

7. Some useful corollaries of the point

1

Who This *All* Means, and in What Order

It is God's prerogative to do good to all; man's ability will not reach to it. But our all is as many as we can do good to.

To Men of All Sorts

To men of all sorts: high and low, rich and poor, old and young, kindred, neighbors, strangers, friends, enemies, good and bad, none excepted that are within our power.

Not to a Few Only

Not to a few only, but to as many persons of all sorts as we can. As he who has true grace would still have more for himself, so he who does good would gladly do more good, and he that does good to some would gladly do good to many more. All good is progressive and tends toward increase and perfection. Why are the faithful said to love and long for the day of Christ's appearing, other than because it is the great marriage day of the Lamb [Rev. 19:6–9], when all the elect shall be perfected in our heavenly society? And that makes it a much more desirable day than that of our particular glorification at death. The perfection of the whole body adds to the perfection of every part, for it is a state of felicity in perfect love. And love makes every man's good whom we love to be as sweet to us as our own—yes, makes it our own. And then the perfection and glory of every saint will be our delight and glory. And to see each single one's love united in one perfect joy and glory will add to each person's joy and glory. And can you wonder if our little sparks of grace do tend toward the same diffused multiplication, and if every member longs for the completing of the body of Christ? O how much will this add to every faithful Christian's joy! It will not be then a little flock, not despised for singularity, nor hidden in the crowd of impious sinners, nor dishonored by infirmities or paltry quarrels among ourselves, nor with the mixture of hypocrites. It will not be oppressed or trod down and persecuted by the power or number of the ignorant enemies. O Christians, go on in doing good to all men with cheerfulness, for it all tends to make up the body of Christ and to prepare for that glorious state and day. Every soul you convert, every brick that you lay in the building, tends to make up the house and city of God.

But as all motion and action is first upon the nearest object, so must ours, and doing good must be in order. First, we must begin at home with our own souls and lives, and next to our nearest relations, friends, acquaintances, and neighbors, and then to our societies, church and kingdom, and all the world. But mark that the order of execution and the order of estimation and intention differ. Though God set up lights so small as will serve but for one room, and though we must begin at home, we must far more esteem and desire the good of multitudes, of city and church and commonwealth, and must set no bounds to our endeavors but what God and disability set.

2

WHAT IS *GOOD*, AND WHAT IS THAT GOOD WHICH WE MUST DO

But what is that good we must do? Good is an attribute of being and is its perfection, or well-being. God's goodness is perfection itself. And as he is the fountain of being, so also of goodness, and therefore his goodness is called love, whose highest act is his essential self-love, which is infinitely above his love for the world. But yet it is communicative love that made all things good and rested in seeing them all good. And as he is the fountain, so the same will, or love, is the measuring rule and the end of all derived good. The prime notion of the creature's goodness is its conformity to the will of God. But the second is its own perfection as its own, which indeed is but the same conformity.

Therefore the true good that we must do men is to make them conformable to the regulating will of God,[1]

---

1. The revealed will of God (*voluntas signi vel praecepti*).

that they may be happy in the pleased will of God,[2] and to help them to all means for soul and body necessary hereunto, and this for as many as we possibly can.

---

2. The hidden will of God (*voluntas decreti vel beneplaciti*).

3

WHAT RULES HE MUST OBSERVE IN DOING IT

The rules for judging and doing good are these:

1. That is the greatest good which is God's greatest interest. And his interest is his glory and the complaisance of his fulfilled will.

2. Therefore the good of the world, the church, of nations, of multitudes is greater than the good of few.

3. The good of the soul is greater than of the body.

4. The avoiding the greatest evil is better than avoiding less.

5. Everlasting good is better than short.

6. Universal good that leaves no evil is better than a particular good.

7. That is the best good, as to means, which most conduces to the end.

8. There is no earthly good that is not mixed with some evil, nor any commodity that has not some inconvenience or discommodity.

9. No sin must be done for any good.

10. Some things may be done for good that would be sin were it not for the good that they are done for. It would be sin to give a robber your money, were it not to save your life or some other commodity. It would be sin to do some things on the Lord's Day that necessity or a greater good may make a duty. Your own defense may make it a duty to strike another, which otherwise would be a sin.

11. In such cases there is need of great prudence and impartiality to know whether the good or the evil do preponderate. And a great part of the actions of our lives must be managed by that prudence or else they will be sinful.

12. Therefore it is no small part of a minister's duty to counsel men as a wise, skillful, and faithful casuist.

4

WHAT QUALIFICATIONS HE MUST HAVE THAT WILL DO GOOD TO MANY

To do good to many requires many excellent qualifications. This is so far from being everyone's performance that we should be glad if a great part of mankind did not do more hurt than good.

He Must Know What Is Good and What Is Bad

He who will do his country good must know what is good and what is bad. A fool's love is hurtful. He knows not how to use it. He will love you to death, as an unskillful physician does his most beloved patients. Or love you into calamity, as amorous lovers often do each other. This is the great enemy of human peace: men know not good from evil, like him who killed his son, thinking he had been a thief, or like routed soldiers who run by mistake into the army of the enemy.

Malignity and error make mad and doleful work in the world, and are worst in those who should be wisest and the greatest instruments of public good. The Scripture is not mistaken that tells us of enemies and haters of God. And most of the world are professed adversaries to Christ. The Jews crucified him as an enemy to Caesar and to the safety of their law and country. And if we may judge by their enmity to holiness, the Spirit of Christ is taken for an intolerable enemy by no small part of nominal Christians. The laws of Christ are judged too strict. The hypocrites who bow to him and hate his laws do call them hypocrites who are but serious in the practice of Christianity, and hate those who have any more religion than compliments, ceremony, and set words. The image of a Christian and a minister is set up in militant opposition to those who are Christians and ministers indeed. If men who are called to the sacred office would save souls in good earnest, and pull them out of the fire, and go any further than pomp and theatrics, they pass for the most insufferable men in the world. Elijah is taken for the troubler of Israel [1 Kings 18:17]; and Paul for a pestilent, seditious fellow [Acts 24:1–9]; and the apostles as the offscouring of all things [1 Cor. 4:13]. Many a martyr has died by fire for seeking to save men from the fire of hell. And when the bedlam world is at this pass, what good is to be expected from such men? When men called Christians hate and oppose the God, the Christ, the Holy Ghost to whom they were vowed in baptism, when drunkenness and whoredom, and perjury and lying, and all debauchery is taken to be friendlier and more tolerable than the most serious worship of God and obedience to his laws and avoiding sin? In a word, when the greatest good is taken for insufferable evil, you may know what good to expect from such.

They will all tell you that we must love God above all and our neighbors as ourselves, but to fight against his word and worship and servants is but an ill expression of their love to God. And seeking their destruction because they will not sin is an ill expression of love to their neighbors. When men judge of good and evil as Satan teaches them and as selfish pride and worldly interest incline them, what wonder if such love has murdered thirty thousand or forty thousand at once in France[1] and two hundred thousand in Ireland[2] and has filled the Christian world with religious blood? Read but the doleful histories of church contentions for thirteen hundred years, the stories of their wars and mutual persecutions, the streams of blood that have been shed in east and west, the inquisitions and bloody laws still kept up, and all this as good works and done in love, and you would think that the sacred Roman hierarchy did believe that Christ had put down the legal sacrificing of beasts that he might instead have the blood of men, and that he who requires his disciples to lay down their lives for him would have a priesthood kept up to sacrifice their lives to him that will not willfully break his laws. And all this is but as Christ foretold us, that his servants should be killed as a piece of service to God [Matt. 24:9]. No wonder if such men offer God a ludicrous, imitative sort of service and worship him in vain by heartless lip service according to the traditions of men, when they dare sacrifice saints to the Lord of saints and quiet their consciences by calling them such as they are themselves. But to the honor of goodness and the shame of sin, to show that they sin against the

---

1. St. Bartholomew's Day massacre, August, 1572.

2. A number commonly circulated at the time in connection with the Irish Rebellion of 1641.

light of nature itself, they put the name of evil upon good before they dare openly oppose and persecute it, and they put the names of good upon evil before they dare defend and justify it.

But alas! It is not only the ungodly who do mischief, thinking verily that it is good. How many does the church suffer by, while they prosecute their mistakes, who yet do much good in promoting the common truth that Christians are agreed in?

He Must Have an Unfeigned Love

He who will do good to all or many must have an unfeigned love for them. Hatred is mischievous, and neglect is unprofitable. Love is the natural fountain of beneficence. Love earnestly longs to do good and delights in doing it. It makes many to be as one and to be as ready to help others as each member of the body is to help the rest. Love makes another's wants, sufferings, and sorrows to be our own. And who is not willing to help himself? Love is a principle ready, active, ingenious, and constant. It studies to do good and would still do more. It is patient with the infirmities of others, which men void of love do aggravate into odiousness and make them their excuse for all their neglects and their pretense for all their cruelties. Could you make all the slanderers, backbiters, revilers, despisers, persecutors to love their neighbors as themselves, you may easily judge what would be the effect, and whether they would revile, or prosecute, or imprison, or ruin themselves, or study how to make themselves odious or suborn perjured witnesses against themselves.

He Must Love Many Better Than Himself

Yes, he who will do good to many must love many better than himself, and prefer the common good much before his own, and seek his own in the common welfare. He who loves good as good will best love the best. And an honest old Roman would have called him an unworthy beast who preferred his estate or life before the common welfare. To be ready to do, suffer, or die for their country was a virtue that all extolled. A narrow-spirited, selfish man will serve others no further than it serves himself or at least will stand with his own safety or prosperity. He will turn as the weathercock and be for those who are for his worldly interest. I confess that God often uses such for common good. But it is by raising such storms as would sink them with the ship and leaving them no great hope to escape by being false or by permitting such villainies as threaten their own interest. A covetous father may be against gaming and prodigality in his children. The men of this world are wise in their generation. Many who have abbey lands will be against popery. And even atheists and licentious men may be loath to be slaves to politic priests and to come under confession and perhaps the Inquisition. And those who have not sinned themselves into madness or gross delusions will be loath to set up a foreign jurisdiction and become the subjects of an unknown priest, if they can help it. God often uses vice against vice, and if no worldly, selfish men were the country's or the church's helpers, it must suffer or trust to miracles.

But yet there is no trust to be put in these men further than their own interest must stand or fall with the common good. If God and heaven and conscience are not more powerful with a man than worldly interest, trust him not against the stream and tide or when he thinks he can make a better bargain for himself. He who will sell heaven and Christ for the world will sell you for it, and sell his country for it, and sell religion, truth, and honesty for it. And if he escapes here the end of Ahithophel [2 Sam. 17:23] and Judas [Matt. 27:5], he will venture on all that's out of sight. Christ was the grand benefactor to the world and the most excellent teacher of love and self-denial and contempt of the world to all who will follow him in doing good to many.

He Must Be Good Himself

He who will do much good must be good himself. Make the tree good if you would have good fruit. *Operari sequitur esse.*[3] A bad man is an enemy to the greatest good that he should do. Malignity abhors serious piety, and will such promote it? If Elijah is a man of miracles, he shall hear, "Have you found me, O my enemy?" [1 Kings 21:20]. And Micaiah shall hear, "I hate him, because he never prophesies good concerning me, but always evil.... Feed him with bread of affliction and water of affliction" [2 Chron. 18:7; 1 Kings 22:27, respectively].

And a bad man, if by accident he is engaged for a good cause, is still suspected by those who know him. They cannot trust him, as being a slave to lust and to strong temptations and a secret enemy to the true interest of his country. Alas! The best are hardly to be trusted far, as being liable to miscarry by infirmity. How little then is to be hoped for from the wicked?

---

3. Doing follows being.

He Must Be Furnished
with Considerable Abilities

He who will do much good in the world must be furnished with considerable abilities, especially prudence, and skill in knowing when, and to whom, and how to do it. Without this he will do more harm than good. Even good men when they have done much good, by a single miscarriage, tempted by the remnants of selfishness and pride and by unskillful rashness, have undone all the good they did and done as much hurt as wicked enemies. There goes so much to public good, and so many snares are to be avoided, that rash, self-conceited, half-witted men do seldom do much, unless under the conduct of wiser men.

He Must Have a Very Large Perspective

He who will be a public blessing to the world must have a very large perspective, and see the state of all the world, and foresee what is likely to come. He must not live as if his neighborhood were all the land or his country, or his party were all the church or all the world. He must know what relation all our actions have to other nations and to all the church of Christ on earth. The want of this universal perspective involves many in censorious and dividing sects who would abhor that way if they knew the case of all the church and world.

And we must not look only to a present exigence or advantage, but foresee how our actions will look hereafter, and what changes may put them under other judgments, and what the fruits may be to posterity. Many things cause death that give the patient present ease.

He Must Have Christian Fortitude

He who will do good to many must have Christian fortitude and not be discouraged with difficulties and opposition. He must serve God for the good of men with absolute resolution and not with the hypocrite's reserve. He must be armed with patience against not only the malice of enemies but the ingratitude of friends. The follies, and quarrels, and mutinies and divisions, and often the abuses of those whom he would do good to must not overcome him. He must imitate God and do good to the evil, and bless those who curse him, and pray for those who spitefully use him. He must not promise himself more success than God has promised him nor yet despair and turn back discouraged. But conscience must carry him on to the end through all, whatever shall befall him.

He Must Look for His Reward from God

Therefore he must look for his reward from God and not expect too much from man. Men are insufficient, mutable, and uncertain. Their interests and many accidents may change them. The multitude are of many minds and tempers, and if you please some, you shall displease others, and it is hard to please even one person long. Some great ones will not be pleased unless you will prefer their wills before the will of God, your country's good, and your own salvation. The poor are so many and so indigent that no man can answer their desires. If you give twenty pounds to twenty of the poor, forty or a hundred who expected the like will murmur at you and be displeased. What man ever did so much good in the world as not to be accused by some as if he were a covetous or a hurtful man?

Therefore, he who will do much good must firmly believe the life to come and must do what he does as the work of God, in obedience to him, and look for his reward in heaven and not as the hypocrite in the praise of men, much less as the worldling in the hope of temporal advantage. He must not wonder if he be rewarded as Socrates was at Athens and as Christ and his apostles were in the world. Themistocles likened himself to a great fruit tree that men run for shelter under in a storm, and when the storm is over they throw stones and cudgels at it to beat down the fruit. Reckon not on a reward from men but from God. By what is said you may perceive what are the great impediments of doing good to many that must be overcome.

1. One, and the worst, is malignity, which is an enmity to spiritual good. For who will promote that which he is against?

2. Another is unbelief in God's commands and promises, when men do not take themselves to be his subject and stewards nor can take his promise for good security for their reward.

3. Another is the aforementioned sin of selfishness, which makes a man's self to be his chief love and care and more to him than Christ's interest, or the church or kingdom.

4. Another is a false conceit that a man is so obliged to provide for his children and kindred that all he can get, however rich he be, must be left to make them rich, except some inconsiderable pittance.

5. Another is the great neglect of parents to prepare their children to be profitable to the commonwealth, but only to live in prosperity for themselves.

   a. Children should be taught, as much as may be, to become persons of understanding, and such wisdom as may make them useful.

   b. And especially to be truly religious. For then they will be devoted to do good, in love and obedience to God.

   c. They should be taught what it is to be members of societies, and what duty they owe to church and state, and how great a part of their duty lies in caring for the common good, and how sinful and damnable it is to live only for themselves, and how much this selfishness is the sum of all iniquity.

   d. Those callings should be chosen for them that they are fittest for and in which they may do most public good.

6. And a fearful, cowardly disposition is a great hindrance to public good. For such will be still for the self-saving way and afraid of the dangers that attend the greatest duties. If they are called to liberality, they will fear lest they should want themselves. In all costly or hazardous duty, there will still be a lion in their way. They cannot trust God, and no wonder then if they are not to be trusted themselves.

7. Lastly, sloth and idleness are constant enemies to well-doing. There are two sorts especially guilty of this.

a. One, and the better, is some religious
people who think that their business
is only with God and their own hearts,
and that if they could spend all their
time in meditation, prayer, and such
like exercises, it would be the best kind
of life on earth. Multitudes among the
papists become friars and nuns by this
conceit. Among us such spend all their
time in hearing sermons, and in reading, and meditating and prayer, and such
like exercises of religion toward God, if
they are but rich enough to live without
bodily labor. And the example of Mary
and Martha [Luke 10:38–42] they think
will make this good.

I know that this is no common error.
The wicked are of a far different mind.
And I know no man can do too much to
save his soul. But we may do one sort
of our work too much to the neglect of
other parts. We have souls in flesh, and
both parts have their proper necessity
and work. Mary did somewhat else than
hear, though she wisely preferred it in its
season. And no one is made for himself
alone. You feel that religious exercises do
you good. But what good is it that you do
to others? I confess a monk's prayer for
others is a good work. But God will have

praying and endeavoring go together, both for yourselves and others. Merely praying God to relieve the poor, and to teach your children, and instruct the ignorant will not excuse you from relieving, teaching, or instructing them. Yes, and your own good will best come in by your fullest obedience to God. Do what he bids you, and he will take care of your salvation. Your own way may seem best, but will not prove best. It will but cast you into melancholy and disability at last; "six days you shall labor" [Ex. 20:9] is more than a permission. It is Saint Paul's canon, "If anyone will not work" if able, "neither shall he eat" [2 Thess. 3:10]. And it was King Solomon's mother who taught him the description of a virtuous woman, who "does not eat the bread of idleness" (Prov. 31:27). God will have mercy and obedience as better than sacrifice [Hos. 6:6; Matt. 12:7]. The sentence in judgment is upon doing good to Christ in his members (Matt. 25:40), when many who heard much and prophesied shall be cast out (Matt. 7:21–23). Doing good is the surest way of receiving good. The duties of the first and second table must go together. He who is not zealous to do good as well as to get good has not the peculiar nature of Christ's flock (Titus 2:14). And zeal will be diligent and not for sloth.

b. The other sort of the idle are rich, ungodly, worldly persons who live as if God did give them plenty for nothing but to pamper their own flesh and feed their own and others' sensuality. They think that persons of wealth and honor may lawfully spend their time in idleness—that is, in Sodom's sin (Ezek. 16:49), as if God expected least where he gives most. How little conscience do many lords and ladies make of an idle hour or life? When poor men's labor is such as tends to the common good, the rich by luxury sacrifice to the flesh the fruits of other men's endeavors, and instead of living in any profitable employment devour that which thousands labor for.

It is not the toilsome drudgery of the common people that we take to be all rich folk's duty. But idleness and unprofitableness is a sin in the richest. Any of them may find good work enough that's fit for them if they are willing. Children, and servants, and friends, and neighbors, and tenants have souls and bodies that need their help. None can say, "God found us no work to do," or that God gave them more time or wealth than they had profitable use for. Little do they think what it will be to reckon for all their time and estates and to be judged according to their works before long. And their own flesh often pays dear for its ease and pleasure by those pains and diseases that God has suited to their sins, and that usually shorten the lives which they no better use, or snatch them away from that time and wealth that they spent in preparing fuel for hell and food for the worm that never dies [Isa. 66:24; Mark 9:48].

5

What Works Must Be Done by Him Who Would Do Good to Many

But what is it a man should do that would do good to all or many? There are some good works that are of far greater tendency than others to the good of many. I will name some of them to you.

Do as Much Good as You Are Able to Men's Bodies

Do as much good as you are able to men's bodies in order to the greater good of souls. If nature be not supported, men are not capable of other good. We pray for our daily bread before pardon and spiritual blessings, not as if it were better, but that nature is supposed before grace, and we cannot be Christians if we are not men. God has so placed the soul in the body that good or evil shall make its entrance by the bodily senses to the soul. God himself conveys many of his blessings this way, and this way he inflicts his corrections. Ministers who are able and willing to be liberal find by great experience that kindness and bounty to men's bodies open their ear to counsel and make them willing to hear instruction. Those in France who are now trying men's religion in the market and are at work with money in one hand and a sword in the other do understand this to be true.[1] All men are sensible of pain or pleasure, good or evil to the flesh, before they are sensible of what is necessary for their souls. You must therefore speak on that side which can hear and work upon the feeling part if you will do good.

Besides this, your charity may remove many great impediments and temptations. It is no easy thing to keep heavenly thoughts upon your mind, and especially to delight in God and keep the relish of his law upon your hearts, while pinching wants are calling away your mind and disturbing it with troublesome passions. To suffer some hunger and go in vile apparel is not very difficult. But when there is a family to provide for, a discontented wife and children to satisfy, rents and debts and demands unpaid, it must be an excellent Christian who can live contentedly and cast all his useless care on God and keep up the sense of his love and a delight in all his service. Do your best to save the poor from such temptations as you would yourselves be saved from them.

And when you give to the poor who are ignorant and ungodly, give them after it some counsel for their souls or some good book that is suited to their cases.

---

1. There were a variety of policies in France under King Louis XIV, who reigned from 1643–1715, intended to promote religious unity. This included financial incentives for those who would convert to Roman Catholicism as well as increasingly coercive measures against Protestants.

Promote the Practical Knowledge of the Truths Necessary to Salvation

If you would do good to many, set yourselves to promote the practical knowledge of the great truths necessary to salvation.

1. Goodness will never be enjoyed or practiced without knowledge. Ignorance is darkness, the state of his kingdom who is the prince of darkness, who by the works of darkness leads the blind world to utter darkness. God is the Father of lights and gives wisdom to those who ask and seek it. He sent his Son to be the light of the world. His word and ministers are subordinate light. His servants are all the children of light. Ignorance is virtually error, and error the cause of sin and misery. And men are not born wise, but must be made wise by skillful, diligent teaching. Parents should begin it. Ministers should second them. But alas! How many millions are neglected by both? And how many neglect themselves when ministers have done their best? Ignorance and error are the common road to wickedness, misery, and hell.

2. But what can any others do for such? Two things I will remind you of:

   a. Set up such schools as shall teach children to read the Scriptures and learn the catechism, or principles of religion. Our departed friend, Mr. Thomas Gouge, did set us an excellent pattern for Wales.[2] I think we have grammar schools enough. It is not the knowledge of tongues and arts and curious sciences that the common people want, but the right understanding of their baptismal covenant with God, and of the Creed, Lord's Prayer, Decalogue, and church communion. For a small stipend a poor honest man or a good woman will teach children thus much better than they are taught it in most grammar schools. And I would none went to the universities without the sound understanding of the catechism. Yes, I would none came thence or into the pulpit without it.

b. When you have got them to read, give them good books, especially Bibles, and good catechisms, and small practical books that press the fundamentals on their consciences. Such books are good catechisms. Many learn the words of the Creed, Lord's Prayer, Commandments, and catechism by rote and never understand them, when a lively book that awakens their consciences brings them to sensible consideration, and to a true understanding of the same things that before they could repeat without sense or

---

2. Thomas Gouge (1605–1681) was a Presbyterian minister, remembered especially for his works of charity. He started setting up schools across Wales in 1674 and helped establish the Welsh Trust, which provided Bibles and other books for these educational efforts.

savor. It is the catechistical truths that most of our English sermons press. And the lively pressing them makes them pierce deeper than a catechism.

If men who in life, or at death, give a stated revenue for good works would settle the one half on a catechizing English school and the other half on some suitable good books, it may prove a very great means of public reformation. When a good book is in the house, if some despise it, others may read it. And when one parish is provided, every year's rent may extend the charity to other parishes, and it may spread over a whole country in a little time. Most of the good that God has done for me, for knowledge or conscience, has been by sound and pious books.

3. A great means of public good is the right ordering of families all the week, but especially on the Lord's Day. Though the ministry be the usual means of converting heathens and infidels, Christian education by parents is the first means appointed by God for the holy instruction of youth. Parents must teach them with unwearied diligence, lying down and rising up (Deut. 6:7). And those who will expect God's blessing must use his appointed means. Nature teaches men and brutes to provide for their offspring with diligence and patience. And as grace teaches believers to expect far greater things for themselves and their children than this world affords, so it obliges them to be at so much greater diligence to obtain it.

An everlasting kingdom deserves more labor than a trade of full estate for the flesh. If all parents did their parts to make their children sanctified believers, as well as they expect the schoolmaster should do his part to make them scholars and the master do his part to teach them their trades, we might hope that ministers would find them fitter for church work, and that godliness would not be so rare, nor so many wicked children break their parents' hearts. But of this I have spoken lately in my *Counsel to Young Men*.[3]

Religion is never likely to prosper if it is not made a family work. If there it is made the chief business of the house and done with reverent seriousness and constancy, if magistracy and ministry should fail, yet families would propagate and preserve it. Begin with a reverent begging the help and blessing of God. Then read his word and call upon his name. Speak serious words of counsel to inferiors. Spend the Lord's Day as much as may be in public worship and the rest in reading godly books and in singing God's praise and calling on his name. Put suitable books into the hands of servants and children to read when they have leisure. Encourage them in it with love and rewards and keep them out of the way of temptation. And then God's blessing will dwell in your families and they will be as

3. *Compassionate counsel to all young men especially I. London apprentices, II. students of divinity, physick, and law, III. the sons of magistrates and rich men* (London: B. Simmons and J. Greenwood, 1681).

churches of God. If any complain of negligent ministers or persecuting magistrates and will not do their own family duties, which none forbids, they condemn themselves.

4. If you would be public blessings and do good to many, do your best to procure a skillful, faithful ministry in the church.

   a. Send no son to the university who does not first show these three qualifications: (1) a capable natural wit and utterance; (2) a love for serious, practical religion; and (3) a great desire to serve God in the ministry, though it should be in suffering from men. If they want any one of these, design them to some other calling. Devote not an undisposed lad to the ministry in hope that God will make him better, but stay till he is better.

   b. Seeing pastors are here obtruded on the flock, it is a work of great importance for religious gentlemen to buy as many advowsons or presentations[4] as they can, that they may introduce the best that they can get.

   God has hitherto made use of the qualifications of the ministers as the special means for the welfare of his church. The mere title and office is so far from sufficing

---

4. The right to recommend or appoint clergy, particularly for a benefice or church stipend. The standard practice was episcopal appointment of pastors rather than the issuing of a call by a congregation.

without the skill and fidelity of the persons that such have been the great corrupters and disturbers of the church. When pious men have heaped up riches and honors on the clergy, these have been baits for the worst men to become seekers and make the sacred ministry but a trade for wealth. And if carnal, worldly men be ministers, alas! What plagues may they be to the people and themselves? They will hate the spiritual practice of doctrine that they preach. When they have told men of a heaven and hell and the necessity of a holy heart and life as if they had been in jest, they will take those for hypocrites who believe them and live accordingly. They will take the best of the flock for their enemies because they are enemies to their hypocrisy and vice. Instead of imitating Saint Paul (Acts 20:18–21), who taught them publicly and from house to house, day and night, with tears, they will turn the ministry into complement and formality and think that by saying a cold, unskillful sermon and by reciting a few heartless words they have laudably performed their part. They will take those for their best hearers who will most honor them and best pay them, though they are ever so ignorant and ungodly. And their spleen will swell against the best and most religious people, because they dislike their unfaithful lives and ministration. If religion should be in public danger, these will be the Judases who will sell it for gain. They will do anything rather than suffer much. They are ministers of the world, and not of Christ, readier to make crosses for others than to bear the cross of Christ. For it is gain that is their godliness. And when their treachery is seen and hated, they will hate the haters of it. And the studies of malignant men will be their laboratories, and the pulpits the place where the sublimate and essence of malice must be vended. How effectually will Satan's work be done when it is performed in the formalities of the sacred ministry and in the name of Christ? O what has the church suffered by a worldly, graceless ministry these thousand years and more, and what does it yet suffer by them in east and west!

But on the other side, a skillful, faithful minister will preach sound doctrine, and worship God with serious devotion, and live for Christ and the church's good. He will speak the word of truth and life, with truth and liveliness, as one who believes what he says and feels the power of it on his heart. Though he must have food and raiment as other men, it is the saving and edifying of souls that is his work, to which he bends all his studies, for which he prays and longs, and in which he rejoices, and to which all his worldly interest not only gives place but is made to serve. He will think no price, no pains or suffering too dear so that the souls of men be saved. This is the riches and preferment which he desires. He has nothing too good or too dear for Christ or for the meanest of his servants when Christ requires it. He is willing to spend and be spent for their sakes. It is *them* and not *theirs* that he desires. He fears the unbelief and hard-heartedness of his hearers and lest they should reject their own salvation more than all the slanders or persecutions of the enemies. In a word: his heart, his study, his life, and business is to do all the good he can. And they who under such a ministry remain impenitent and hardened in sin are the most hopeless, miserable people in the world.

5. And it greatly conduces to public good to keep up true order and Christian discipline in the particular churches. Though popish church tyrants have turned the church keys into a military reigning or revenging sword, yet Christ did not in vain commit them into his ministers' hands. Religion seldom prospers well where the church is no enclosure, but a common where all sorts, undistinguished, meet. Where, as the people know not who shall be made their pastors but must trust their souls to the care of any a patron chooses, so the pastor knows not who are his communicating flock until he sees them come to the Lord's Table, no, nor when he sees them. When it goes for a sufficient excuse to the pastors if the rabble of wicked men communicate, or pass for his church members, though they communicate not, if he can but say, "I knew them not

to be wicked" (and how should he, when he knew them not at all?), and that "none accused them," when they are meet strangers to each other. In Christ Jesus neither circumcision nor uncircumcision avails anything, but a new creature and faith that works by love [Gal. 5:6; 6:15]. And if Christ made his servants no better than the world, who would believe that he is the Savior of the world? There will be some tares in Christ's field until his judgment cast them out forever. But if it be not a society professing holiness and disowning unholiness, and making a difference between the clean and the unclean, him that swears and him that fears an oath, him that serves God and him that serves him not, then Christ will disown them as workers of iniquity, though they had eaten and drank with him and done miracles in his name (Matt. 7:21–23). Much more if it be a society where godliness is despised and the most godly excommunicated, if they differ but in a formality or ceremony from Diotrephes [3 John 9–10], and the wicked rabble tolerated and cherished in reviling serious godliness on pretense of opposing such dissenters. Christ will not own that pastor or society which owns not conscience and serious piety.

If the pastors set up their wills and traditions before the laws and will of Christ and call out, "Who is on our side?" instead of, "Who is on Christ's side?" and fall out with the sheep and worry and scatter them, and cherish the goats, and tolerate the wolves, woe to those shepherds when Christ shall judge them. I wonder not if such incline to infidelity, though they live by the name and image of Christianity, and if they are loath to believe that there will be such a day of judgment, which they have so much cause to fear.

But the prudent, loving guidance of faithful pastors is so necessary to the church that without it there will be envy and strife, confusion, and every evil work. And a headless multitude, though otherwise well-meaning, pious people, will be all wise, and all teachers, until they have no wise teachers left, and will crumble all into dissolution or into shameful sects. Saint Paul told us of two games that Satan has to play (Acts 20:29–30). One by "savage wolves" that shall devour the flock (though in sheep's clothing, yet known by their bloody jaws). The other by men "from among yourselves" who "will rise up, speaking perverse things, to draw away the disciples after themselves."

6. If you would promote the good of all or many, promote the love and concord of all who deserve to be called Christians.

To which end you must: (a) Know who those are, and (b) skillfully and faithfully endeavor it.

a. Far be it from any Christian to think that Christ has not so much as told us what Christianity is and who they be that we must take for Christians, when he has commanded them all so earnestly to love each other. Is not baptism our christening? Everyone who has entered into that covenant with Christ, and understandingly and seriously professes to stand to it, and is not proved by inconsistent words or deeds to nullify that profession is to be taken for a Christian and treated in love and communion as such.

Consider these words, and consider whether all churches have walked by this rule, and whether swerving from it has not been the cause of corruption and confusion.

He is a Christian fit for our communion who is baptized in infancy and owns it solemnly at age. And so is he who was not baptized until he himself believed.

He is a Christian who believes Christ to be true God and true man in one person, and trusts him as our only Redeemer by his merits and passion, and our Mediator in the heavens, and obeys him as our sovereign Lord for pardon, for his Spirit, and for salvation. And as a Christian this man is to be loved and treated, though he have not so much skill in metaphysics as to know whether it be a proper speech to call Mary the mother of God, or that one of the Trinity was crucified, or to know in what sense Christ's natures might be called one or two, and in what sense he might be said to have one will or two wills, one operation or two, and know not whether the *tria capitula* were to be condemned, yes, though he could not define or clearly tell what *hypostasis*, *persona*, yes, or *substantia* signifies in God, nor tell whether "God of gods" be proper speech.[5]

This man is a Christian, though he know not whether patriarchal, and metropolitical, and diocesan church forms be according to the will of Christ or against it, and whether symbolical signs in the worship of God may lawfully be devised and imposed by men, and whether some doubtful words in oaths and subscriptions of men's imposing, being unnecessary, are lawful, and how far he may by them incur the guilt of perjury or deliberate lying, and though he think that a minister may preach and pray in fit words of his own, though he read not a sermon or prayer written for him by others who think that no words but theirs should be offered to God or man.

b. If Christ's description of a Christian be forsaken, and mere Christianity seem not a sufficient qualification for our love and concord, men will never know where to rest, nor ever agree in anyone's determination but Christ's. All men who can get power will be making their own wills the rule and law, and others will not think of them as they do, and the variety of fallible mutable church laws and terms of concord will be the engine

---

5. The preceding are references to a variety of Christological debates in the early church that were the source of great controversy, culminating in decisions from major ecumenical councils and the formulation of creedal orthodoxy.

of perpetual discord (as Ulpian told honest Severus Alexander the laws would be, which he thought to have made for sober concord, in fashions of apparel).[6] Those who are united to Christ by faith, and have his sanctifying Spirit, and are justified by him, and shall dwell with him in heaven are certainly Christians, and such as Christ has commanded us to love as ourselves. And seeing that it is his livery by which his disciples must be known by loving one another, and the false prophets must be known by the fruits of their hurtfulness as wolves, thorns, and thistles, I must profess, though order and government have been so amiable to me as to tempt me to favorable thoughts of some Roman power in the church, I am utterly irreconcilable to it when I see that the very complexion of that hierarchy is malice and bloodiness against men most seriously and humbly pious who dare not obey them in their sinful usurpations, and that their cause is maintained by belying, hating, and murdering true Christians.

And on the other side, too many make laws of love and communion to themselves and confine Christ's church with their little various and perhaps erroneous sects. And all others they love with pity,

---

6. Ulpian (c. 170–223 AD) was a famed Roman jurist who held the praetorian prefecture, the largest administrative division of government, under emperor Severus Alexander (c. 207–235 AD).

but only those of their cabin and singular opinions they love with complacency and communion. Those who condemn such as Christ justifies and say that Christians are not his are near of kin to one another, though one sort show it by persecution, and the other but by excommunication or schismatic separation. "We are all one in Christ Jesus" (Gal. 3:28). And therefore I advise all Christians to hate the causes and ways of hatred, and love all the causes and means of love. Frown on them who so extol their singular sentiments as to backbite others and speak evil of what they do not understand. Especially such as the pamphleteers of this age, whose design is weekly and daily to fight against Christian love and to stir up all men to the utmost of their power to think odiously of one another and plainly to stir up a thirst after blood. Never did Satan write by the hand of man if he does it not by such as these. The Lord of love and mercy rebuke them.

And take heed of those who can find enough in the best that are against their way to prove them dishonest, if not intolerable, and can see the mote of a ceremony, or nonconformity to a ceremony, in their brother's eye and not the beam of malice or cruelty in their own. Take heed of those who are either for confounding toleration of all or for dissipating cruelty on pretense of unity.

That land or church shall never truly prosper where these three sorts are not well distinguished: (1) The *approved*, who are to be encouraged; (2) the *tolerable*, who are to be patiently and lovingly endured; and (3) the *intolerable*, who are to be restrained. They may as well confound men and beasts, wise men and madmen, adults and infants, as confound these three sorts in reference to religion.

I add this note to prevent objections, that though meekness and gentleness promote peace, yet to speak sharply and hatefully of hatred, unpeaceableness, and cruelty, and all that tends to destroy love, is an act of love and not of an uncharitable, unpeaceable man.

7. If you love the common good of England, do your best to keep up sound and serious religion in the public parish churches and be not guilty of anything that shall bring the chief interest of religion into private assemblies of men that are only tolerated, if you can avoid it.

Indeed, in a time of plagues and epidemical infection, tolerated churches may be the best preservatives of religion, as it was in the first three hundred years, and in the Arians' reign, and under popery. But where sound and serious religion is owned by the magistrate, tolerated churches are but as hospitals for the sick and must not be the receptacle of all the healthy. And doubtless, if the papists can but get the Protestant interest once into prohibited or tolerated conventicles (as they will call them), they have more than half overcome it and will not hesitate to use it next as they do in France, and by one turn more to cast it out. The countenance of authority will go far with the common people against all the scruples that men of conscience stick at, and they will mostly go to the allowed churches, whoever is there. Let us therefore lose no possession that we can justly get, nor be guilty of disgracing the honest conformists, but do all we can to keep up their reputation, for the good of souls. They see not matters of difference through the same glass that we do. They think us unwarrantably scrupulous. We think the matter of their sin to be very great. But we know that before God the degree of guilt is much according to the degree of men's negligence or unwillingness to know the truth or to obey it. And prejudice, education, and converse make great difference for men's apprehensions. Charity must not reconcile us to sin, but there is no end of uncharitable censuring each other.

It has made me admire to hear some men's words against comprehension, as they call it, that they would not have rulers revoke that which they judge to be heinous sin in their impositions, unless they will revoke all that they think unlawful, lest it should strengthen the parish churches and weaken the tolerated or suffering part.[7] I will not here open the sin

---

7. The debate over comprehension, which would allow for greater diversity within the Anglican church, or toleration, which would exclude dissenters from formal status within the estab-

of this policy as it deserves. But I wish them
to read a small book called *The Whole Duty of
Nations* (said to be Mr. Thomas Beverley's).[8]

8. If you love the common good, take heed
lest any injuries tempt you into sedition or
unlawful wars. No man who never tried them
can easily believe what an enemy wars and
tumults are to religion and to common honesty and sobriety. Men are there so serious
about their lives and bodily safety that they
have no room or time for serious worshiping
of God. The Lord's Day is by necessity made a
common day. And all men's goods are almost
common to the will of soldiers. Either power
seems to authorize them, or necessity to allow
them, to use the goods of others as their own,
as if they were incapable of doing wrong. It is
their honor that can kill most, and how little
place there is for love it is easy to conceive.

I doubt not but it is lawful to fight for our
king or country in a good cause. As nature
gives all private men a right of private self-
defense (and no more), so the same law of
nature, which is God's law, gives all nations a
right of public self-defense against their public enemies—that is, against any that by his
religion or his own profession binds himself
to destroy that nation if he can, or by open

---

lishment, was a key feature of seventeenth-century religious
controversy in England.

8. Thomas Beverley, *The whole duty of nations; or, National
true religion argued and perswaded upon greatest motives of
Scripture and reason* (London: Tho. Parkhurst, 1681).

arms seeks no less than their destruction. But as few calamities are worse to a land than war, so much is to be endured to prevent it. It is like a red-hot iron that fools lay hold on, thinking it is gold, until it fetches off skin and flesh to the bones and perhaps sets the house on fire. If your cause is bad, God will not be for you, and he that so takes the sword shall perish with the sword [Matt. 26:52]. And if you bite and devour one another, you shall be devoured one of another [Gal. 5:15]. And, alas, thousands of the innocent usually perish or are ruined in the flames that furious men do kindle. No doubt as suffering a prison, so venturing in war is a duty when God calls you to it. But in itself a prison is a far more desirable sort of suffering than a war. Therefore, between the danger of the miseries of an unlawful war and the danger of betraying our king or kingdom for want of necessary defense, how cautious should all sober Christians be?

9. If you would promote the common good, do your best to procure wise and faithful rulers.

Question: What can private men do in this?

Answers:

a. In cases where they have choosing voices, they ought to prefer the best with greatest resolution, and not for slothfulness to omit their part, nor for worldly interest or the fear of men betray their country, as ever they would escape the punishment of the perfidious. Woe to that Judas who sells his country and conscience for any bribe, or by self-saving fear.

b. In other cases where you have no choosing vote with men, you have a praying voice with God. Pray for kings and all in authority that we may live a quiet and peaceable life, in all godliness and honesty [1 Tim. 2:2]. God has commanded no duty in vain. Do it earnestly and constantly, and hope for a good issue from God. Do it not selfishly that you may have prosperity or preferment by them, but sincerely for their own and the common good. God is the fountain of power, the absolute sovereign of all the world. Men are but his provincial officers. None claims a universal government of the world except one who pretends to be Christ's vicar-general, and none believe his claim but blinded men. There is no power but of and under God, who has made rulers his ministers for our good, to be a praise to them who do well and a terror to evildoers [Rom. 13:3–4], that they who will not be moved with the hopes of God's future rewards and the fears of his punishments may be moved by that which is near them within the reach of sense. And all men regard their bodies, though only believers are ruled by the everlasting interest of their souls.

Therefore, pray hard for kings and magistrates. For if they be good, they are exceedingly great blessings to the world. They will remember that their power is for God and the common good, and that to God they must give a strict account. They will take God's law for the only universal law to the world, and conform their own as by-laws to it. They will take their own interest to consist in pleasing God, and promoting the gospel and kingdom of Christ, and the piety and saving of men's souls. They will be examples of serious godliness, of justice and sobriety, trustiness and temperance and chastity to their subjects. In their eyes a vile person will be condemned, but they will honor those who fear the Lord (Ps. 15:4). They will love those most who love Christ best, and most diligently obey him, and tenderly fear to sin against him. Those please them best who please God best, and are most useful to the common good. They will set their hearts on the people's welfare and are watching for all, while all securely live under their vigilance. They will cherish all that Christ cherishes, and especially the faithful pastors of the churches who seek not the world, but the welfare of the flocks. When some are saying, "On this mountain we must worship God," and some, "At Jerusalem," they will teach them all to worship God in Spirit and truth [John 4:20, 24]. When pastors and people grow peevish and quarrelsome for their several interests, opinions, and wills, a Constantine will cast all their libels into the fire, and rebuke the unpeaceable, and restrain the violent, and teach them to forgive and love each other, and will be the great justice of peace to all the churches in the land, and pare their nails that would tear and scratch their brethren. He will countenance the sound and peaceable and tolerate all the tolerable, but will tie the hands of strikers and the tongues of revilers. He will contrive the healing of exasperated minds, and take away the occasions of division, and rebuke them that call for fire from heaven, or for the sword to do that which belongs to the word, or to execute their pride and wrath. Godliness will have all the encouragement they can give it, and innocence a full defense. Malignity and persecution and perjury and unpeaceable revenge will be hateful where they rule, and they had rather men feared sin too much than too little, and would have all men prefer the law and honor of God to theirs. Where the righteous bear authority, the people rejoice [Prov. 29:2]. The wisdom, piety, and impartiality of their governors suppress profaneness, oppression, and contention and keep men in the way of love and peace. And as the welfare of all is the care of such a ruler above his own pleasure, wealth, or will, so he will have the hearts and hands and wealth of all with readiness to serve him. No wonder if such are called nursing fathers [Isa. 49:23 KJV], and the light of our eyes, and

the breath of our nostrils [Lam. 4:20], and
the shadow of a rock in a weary land [Isa.
32:2]. As they bear the image of God's
supereminence and doubly honor him,
they are doubly honored by him, so that
the names of pious princes show not only
the sense of mankind but the special prov-
idence of God in making the memory of
the just to be blessed [Prov. 10:7]. And as
they could not endure to see in their days
ungodliness triumph, or serious godliness
made a scorn, or conscience and fear of
sinning made a disgrace, or the gospel
hindered and faithful ministers forbidden
to preach it, so God will not suffer their
consciences to want the sense of his love,
nor their departing souls to fail of their
everlasting hopes, nor their memories to
be clouded by obscurity or reproach. Even
among heathens, what a name have those
emperors left behind them, who lived in
justice, charity, and all virtue, and wholly
studied the good of all? What a wonder
is it that Antoninus should be so extolled
by so many writers, and not one of them
all, that I remember, speak one word of
evil of him, save that a small and short
persecution of the Christians was made
by some in his time, until he restrained
it?[9] And all the people almost deified him
and would have perpetuated his line and
name in the throne, but that the horrid

---

9. Roman emperor Antoninus Pius (86–161 AD), famed for the
peace and tranquility enjoyed during his reign.

wickedness of his posterity forced them to a change. What a name has excellent Severus Alexander left behind him? And what a blessing have wise and godly and peacemaking Christian princes been in diverse ages to the world?

And both the inferior magistrates and the clergy usually much conform themselves, at least in outward behavior, to their example. For they will choose men of wisdom, conscience, and justice under them to judge and govern. The bishops and pastors whom they choose will be able, godly, laborious men, not seekers of worldly wealth and honor, not envious silencers of faithful preachers, nor jealous hinderers of religious duties, nor flattering man-pleasers, nor such as lord it over God's heritage, but such as rule not by constraint, but willingly, as examples of love and piety to the flock [1 Pet. 5:1–3]. Pray hard therefore for kings and all in authority, and honor all such as unspeakable blessings for the good of all.

But on the contrary, wicked rulers will be Satan's captains against Jesus Christ and men's sanctification and salvation. They will be wolves in the place of shepherds, and will study to destroy the best of the people, and to root out all serious godliness and justice. Conscience and fearing sin will be to them a suspected, yes, a hated thing. If any abuse it, it serves them for a pretense against it. They take the people's welfare and their own interest to be enemies, and presently look on these whom they should rule and cherish as the adversaries whom they must tread down. They will purposely make edicts and laws that are contrary to God's law, that they may have advantage to persecute the faithful and to destroy them as disobedient. They will study to conquer conscience and obedience to God, lest his authority should be regarded above theirs, and Christ is used by them as if he were a usurper, and not their sovereign, but were again to be taken for an enemy to Caesar, and their hatred to true ministers will be such as Paul's accusers intimate, who said he preached "another king—Jesus" [Acts 17:7]. Wicked rulers will be the capital enemies to all who will be enemies to wickedness and resolved to please God and save their souls. They will not be obeyed under God, but before him, nor served by the faithful servants of Christ, nor pleased, but at the rate of men's damnation by displeasing God. All men love their like. The worst men, if flatterers, will seem the best to them, and the best the worst and most intolerable. And church and state are like to be written by their copy. O what dreadful plagues have wicked rulers been to the world, and what a dismal case do they continue the earth in to this day! Not but that people, and especially priests, do contribute hereto. But the chief authors are men in greatest power.

Five parts of six of the world at this day are heathens and infidels. And what's the cause? Rulers will not suffer the gospel to be preached to them. The Eastern Christians were all torn in pieces by the wickedness and contention of the governors of the state and church, banishing and murdering one another, so that when the Turks invaded them, the promise of liberty to exercise their religion tempted them to make the less resistance, thinking they could not be much worse than before. But the common people are so apt to follow the rulers that ever since, most of the Easterns are apostatized from Christ and turned to Islam. And though religion somewhat prospers in those countries where the Turk allows the Christian people to have governors of their own, yet where that privilege is denied them and Turks only are their rulers, it withers away and comes to almost nothing.

And what keeps out reformation—that is, the primitive, simple Christianity—from the popish countries that have religion corrupted by human superfluities, but the seduction of priests and the tyranny of rulers that will not endure the preaching of the gospel and the opening of the Scriptures to the people in a known tongue? How much holy blood have Roman and Spanish inquisitors, and French and Irish murderers, and most other popish rulers to answer for? Even

Walsh the papist, in his Irish history,[10] tells us all, out of Keating[11] and others, how commonly in ages they lived there in the sin of bloody wars and murders— yes, even when they professed greatest holiness. Wicked rulers are as the pikes in the pond that live by devouring all about them. It is Satan's main design in the world to corrupt God's two great ordinances of magistracy and ministry, and turn them both against Christ's kingdom, and to destroy Christians in Christ's name. Oh! Therefore, pray hard that all Christian nations may have good rulers, and be very thankful to God for such.

10. And if you would be instruments of public good, know what are public sins and dangers, that you may do your part against them, and join not with any who will promise never to endeavor any reforming alteration. The chief are ignorance, pride, and self-willedness in teachers and people, malignant enmity to goodness, impatience with the infirmities of good men, judging of persons and things by self-interest, covetousness, sensuality, and taking Christianity but as the religion of the land without diligent study to be rooted in the truth. And the scandals of

---

10. Peter Valesius Walsh, O.F.M. (c. 1618–1688), author of works including *A prospect of the state of Ireland from the year of the world 1756 to the year of Christ 1652* (London: Johanna Broom, 1682).

11. Seathrún Céitinn (c. 1569–c. 1644), an Irish historian, priest, and poet, known in English as Geoffrey Keating (Ketin in Baxter's original).

hypocrites and tempted Christians, hardening the enemies, especially by divisions and public temerities and miscarriages, are not the least.

11. I would also, in order to public good, persuade serious Christians to be more zealous in communication with their neighbors, and live not over-strangely to others, and say not as Cain, "Am I my brother's keeper?" [Gen. 4:9]. Be kind and loving to all about you, and live not as unknown men to them, nor alienate them by sourness, contempt, or needless singularity. But become all things lawful to all men to save some [1 Cor. 9:22]. Lend them good books, and draw them to hear God's faithful ministers. Persuade them to pray in their families, even with a form or book, until they need it not.

12. Lastly, if you would do good, be such as you would have others be, and teach them by examples of piety, charity, patience, self-denial, forbearing, and forgiving, and not by mere words contradicted by your lives. These are the materials by which you must do good to all.

6

WHAT MOTIVES SHOULD QUICKEN US TO THE PRACTICE

What Remains for Us

What now remains but that we all set ourselves to such a fruitful course of life? I greatly rejoice in the grace of God, which I daily see in many such of my familiar acquaintance, who study to do good to all and to live in love and peace and holiness by example and by self-denial and constant charity, using Christ's talents to their master's ends, for the temporal and eternal good of many. But alas! Too many live as if it were enough to do no harm and say as the slothful servant, "Here is your talent which I hid" [Matt. 25:25].

And some there be that in a blind jealousy of the doctrine of justification (not understanding what the word *justification* signifies) cry down even the words of James, as if they were irreconcilable with Paul's, and can scarce bear him who says as Christ, "For by your words you will be justified, and by your words you will be condemned" (Matt. 12:37). As if they had never read,

"Well done, good and faithful servant" [Matt. 25:23], and "for I was hungry and you gave Me food" [Matt. 25:35]. Nor Hebrews 5:9: "He became the author of eternal salvation to all who obey Him." Or Hebrews 13:16: "for with such sacrifices God is well pleased." Or "he who practices righteousness is righteous" [1 John 3:7]. Or "they were judged, each one according to his works" [Rev. 20:13]. Or Revelation 22:14: "Blessed are those who do His commandments, that they may have the right to the tree of life, and may enter through the gates into the city." Or Galatians 6:7–8: "For whatever a man sows, that he will also reap.... He who sows to the Spirit will of the Spirit reap everlasting life," and many such passages.

No man in his right mind can think that anything we do can merit of God in commutative justice, as if he received anything from us. This were even to deny God to be God. But are we not under a law of grace, and does not that law command us obedience and the improvement of our talents in doing good? And shall we not be judged by that law? And what is judging but justifying or condemning? No works of ours can stand the trial by the law of innocence or works, but only the perfect righteousness of Christ. But he who is accused of final impenitency, infidelity, hypocrisy, or unholiness, if truly accused, shall never be justified, and if falsely, he must be justified against that charge by somewhat besides what is done out of him by Jesus Christ.

It is an easier thing to be zealous for an opinion (that is sound or supposed such) about works and grace than to be zealous of good works or zealously desirous of grace. How sad use did Satan make of men's zeal for orthodox words when the Nestorian, Eutychian, and Monothelite controversies were in agitation?[1] He went for an insin-

---

1. Christological heresies of the early church.

cere neutral party that did not hereticate one side or other. And I would that factious, ignorant zeal were not still alive in the churches. How many have we heard on one side reviling Lutherans, Calvinists, Arminians, Episcopals, Presbyterians, Independents, and so on, to render them odious, who never understand the true state of the difference? And how fiercely do some papists and others cry down Solifidians,[2] and persuade men that we are enemies to good works, or think that they are not necessary to salvation (because some rashly maintained that in a faction against George Major[3] long ago), or at least that they are no further necessary but as signs to prove that which God knows without them? And on the other side, how many make themselves and others believe that the true expositors of Saint James's words are almost papists and teach men dangerously to trust to works for their justification, while they understand not what either of the apostles mean by justification, faith, or works. Many so carefully avoid trusting to good works that they have none or few to trust to. No doubt nothing of man must be trusted to for the least part that belongs to Christ. But all duty and means must be both used and trusted for their own part.

---

2. An epithet used to describe those who affirm justification by faith alone (*sola fide*).

3. Georg Major (1502–1574) was a Lutheran theologian whose teachings were at the center of the so-called Majoristic controversy over the relationship between faith, works, and salvation.

Consider well these following motives, and you will see why all Christians must be zealous of doing all the good they can.

1. It renders a man alike to God to be good and to do good, on which account Christ requires it even toward our enemies (Matt. 5:43–48), that we may "be perfect, just as your Father in heaven is perfect," who does good even to the unjust. And he who is most like God is the best man, most holy and most happy, and shall have most communion with God.

2. And when Christ came down in flesh to call man home by making God better known to the world, he revealed him in his attractive goodness, and that was by his own beneficence to man. He came to do the greatest good, to be the Savior of the world, and to reconcile revolted man to God, and all his life—yes, his death and his heavenly intercession—is doing good to those who were God's enemies. And to learn of Christ and imitate his example is to be his true disciples. And what else do his laws command us? They are all holy, just, and good, and our goodness is to love them and obey them. By keeping these we must show that we are his disciples. When he tells you who you must do good to in the instance of the Samaritan, he adds, "Go and do likewise" (Luke 10:37). He tells us at length of what importance it is for every branch that is planted into him to bring forth fruit.

3. It is much of the end of all the sanctifying operations of the Holy Spirit. Grace is given us to use. Even natural powers are given us for action. What the better were man for a tongue, or hands, or feet if he should never use them? Life is a principle of action. It would be as good to have no life as not to use it. And why does God make men good, but that they may do good, even in their duty to God, themselves, and one another?

4. It is God's great mercy to mankind that he will use us all in doing good to one another. And it is a great part of his wise government of the world that in societies men should be tied to it by the sense of every particular man's necessity. And it is a great honor to those who he makes his almoners or servants to convey his gifts to others. God bids you give nothing but what is his, and no otherwise your own than as his stewards. It is his bounty and your service or stewardship which is to be exercised. He could have done good to all men by himself alone, without you or any other, if he would. But he will honor his servants to be the messengers of his bounty. You best please him when you readily receive his gifts yourselves and most fully communicate them to others. To do good is to receive good. And yet he will reward such for doing and receiving.

5. Self-love, therefore, should persuade men to do good to all. You are not the least gainers by it yourselves. If you can trust Christ, surely you will think this profitable usury. Is not a cup of

cold water well paid for, when Christ performs his promise? And is it not a gainful loss, which is rewarded in this life a hundredfold and in the world to come with life eternal?

Those who live in the fullest exercise of love and doing good are usually most loved, and many are ready to do good to them. And this exercise increases all fruitful graces. And there is a present delight in doing good, which is itself a great reward. The love of others makes it delightful to us. And the pleasing of God, and the imitation of Christ, and the testimony of conscience make it delightful. An honest physician is far gladder to save men's lives or health than to get their money. And an honest soldier is gladder to save his country than to get his pay. Every honest minister of Christ is far gladder to win souls than to get money or preferment. The believing giver has more pleasure than the receiver, and this without any conceit of commutative meriting of God or any false trust to works for justification.

6. Stewards must give account of all. What would you wish were the matter of your true account if death or judgment were tomorrow? Would you not wish you had done all the good you could? Do you believe that all shall be judged according to their works? Did you ever well study that great prediction of Christ (Matt. 25)?

And it is some part of a reward on earth that men who do much good, especially that to whole nations, are usually honored by posterity, however they be rewarded by the present age.

7. Every true Christian is absolutely devoted to do good. What else is it to be devoted to God our Creator and Redeemer? What do we live for, or what should we desire to live for, but to do good?

To Those Who Have Special Opportunity

But this exhortation is especially applicable to those who have special opportunity.

1. Magistrates are the leaders in the societies and public affairs of mankind. They are placed highest that they may have a universal influence. Though it be too high a word to call them gods, or God's vicegerents (unless *secundum quid*),[4] yet they are his officers and regent ministers; but it is for the common good. In them God shows what order can do in the government of the world. As the placing of the same figure before many does accordingly advance its value in signification, so it is a wonder to note what the place of one man signifies at the head of an army, of a city, of a kingdom. They are appointed by God to govern men in a just subordination to God's government, and no otherwise; to promote obedience to God's laws by theirs, and by their judgment and execution to give men a foretaste of what they may at last expect from God; and

---

4. That is, in a qualified sense.

by their rewards and punishments to foretell men whom God will reward and punish; and by their own examples to show the subjects how temperately and soberly and godly God would have them live. Atheists who do not fear God because they do not know him can see and fear a magistrate.

They who prefer those as the most worthy of honor whom God abhors for their wickedness, and hate and oppress those whom God will honor, do show themselves enemies to him that gives them all their power. And they who by countenance or practice do teach men to despise the fear of God and to make light of drunkenness, whoredom, lying, perjury, and such like odious crimes do in a sort blaspheme God himself, as if he who exalted them were a lover of sin and a hater of his own laws and service. There are few rulers who are unwilling of power or to be accounted great. And do they not know that it is a power to do good that God has given them? And that obligation to do it is as essential to their office as authority? And that they who govern as the officers of God and pretend to be more like him in greatness than their subjects must also be more like to him in wisdom and goodness?

Woe to that man who abuses and oppresses the just and faithful in the name of God, and does so by pretense of authority from him. Woe to him who in God's name, and as by his authority, countenances the wicked whom God abhors and under Christ's banner fights against him. As Christ says of the offensive:

It would have been good for that man if he had not been born [Matt. 26:24].

He who says to the wicked, "You are righteous,"
Him the people will curse;
Nations will abhor him. (Prov. 24:24)

He who justifies the wicked, and he who condemns the just, both of them alike are an abomination to the Lord (Prov. 17:15).

God looks for great service from great men. Great trust and talents must have great account. A prince, a lord, a ruler must do much more good in promoting piety, conscience, virtue than the best inferiors. To whom men give much, from them they expect the more. It greatly concerns such men seriously to ask their conscience, "Can I do no more to encourage godliness, conscience, and justice, and to disgrace malignity, brutish sensuality, and fleshly lusts, than I have done?" O when they must hear, "Give an account of your stewardship, for you can no longer be steward" [Luke 16:2], many rulers think little what an account it is that will be required of them! O what a deal of good may the rulers of the earth do if, instead of worrying over their partial interests and serving the desires of the flesh, they did but set themselves with study and resolution to promote the common good by disgracing sin and encouraging wisdom, piety, and peace! And where this is not sincerely done, as surely as there is a righteous God and a future judgment, they shall pay for their omissive treachery. And if Satan does prevail to set his own captains over the armies of the Lord to betray them to perdition, they shall be deepest in misery as they were in guilt. One would think the great delight that is to be found in doing good to all should much more draw men to desire authority and greatness than either riches, or voluptuousness, or a domineering desire that all men should fulfill their wills.

2. The ministers of Christ also have the next opportunity to do good to many. And it is a debt that by many and great obligations they owe to Christ and men. But it will not be done without labor and condescension and unwearied patience. It is undertaken by all who are ordained to this office, but O that it were performed faithfully by all! What a doleful life would the perfidious soul-betrayers live if they knew what a guilt they have to answer for! Even the contempt of the people's souls and of the blood of Christ that purchased them! O hear that vehement adjuration: "I charge you therefore before God and the Lord Jesus Christ, who will judge the living and the dead at His appearing and His kingdom: Preach the word! Be ready in season and out of season. Convince, rebuke, exhort, with all longsuffering and teaching" (2 Tim. 4:1–2). Speak with holy studied skill. Speak with love and melting pity. Speak with importunity. Take no denial. Speak as Saint Paul, "publicly and from house to house" (Acts 20:20). Speak before you are silenced in the dust. Speak before death has taken away your hearers. It is for souls; it is for Christ; it is for yourselves too. While you

have opportunity, do good to all. But of this I have formerly said more in my *Reformed Pastor*.[5]

3. And let all men take their common and special opportunities to do good. Time will not stay. Yourselves, your wives, your children, your servants, your neighbors are posting to another world. Speak now what you would have them hear. Do them now all the good you can. It must be now or never. There is no returning from the dead to warn them. O live not as those infidels who think it enough to do no harm and to serve their carnal minds with pleasure, as born for nothing but a decent and delightful life on earth. You are all in the vineyard or harvest of the Lord. Work while it is day. The night is at hand when none can work [John 9:4]. Woe to the slothful, treacherous hypocrite when the judgment comes!

Do not wait till you are entreated to do good. Study it and seek it. Give while there are men who need, and while you have it, especially to the household of faith. Fire and thieves may deprive you of it. At the furthest, death will quickly do it. Happy are they who know their day and, trusting in Christ, do study to serve him in doing good to all.

---

5. *Gildas Salvianus, the reformed pastor shewing the nature of the pastoral work, especially in private instruction and catechizing* (London: Robert White, 1656).

7

SOME USEFUL COROLLARIES OF THE POINT

And the doctrine in hand does further teach us some corollaries that all do not well consider.

The Difference between a Hypocrite and a Sound Christian

That living chiefly to the flesh in worldly prosperity, and dropping now and then occasionally some small good to quiet conscience, is the property of a hypocrite. But to sound Christians, fruitfulness in doing good is the very trade of their lives, of which they are zealous, and which they daily study.

Be Careful to Avoid Doing Public Hurt

That all Christians should be very careful to avoid doing public hurt. It wounds conscience to be guilty of wronging of any one man. We find it in dying men who cannot die in peace till they have confessed wrongs and made satisfaction and ask forgiveness. And who knows but the many apparitions that have certainly been seen on such occasions may have been imagined by miserable souls to seek some ease of the torment of their own consciences? But to hurt many—even whole parishes, cities, churches, kingdoms—how much more grievous will it prove? And yet alas! How quickly may it be done, and how ordinarily is it done? What grievous mischief may even well-meaning men do by one mistaken practice or rash act? By the fierce promoting of one error? By letting loose one passion or carnal affection? By venturing once on secret sin? Yes, by one rash, sinful word? How much more if they are drawn and set in an unlawful interest and way? And little know we when a spark is kindled how it will end? Or how many ways Satan has to stoke it? And one hurtful action or unwarrantable way may blast abundance of excellent endowments and make such a grievous damage to the church, which else might have been an eminent blessing. And if good men may do so much hurt, what have the enemies of godliness to answer for, who by wordliness and malignity are corrupters, dividers, and destroyers?

Do Not Leave the Doing of Good to Your Estate's Executors

The text plainly intimates that it is a great crime in those that, instead of doing good while they have opportunity, think it enough to leave it by will to their executors to do it. When they have lived to the flesh and cannot take it with them, they think it enough to leave others to do that good which they had not a heart to do themselves. But a treasure must be laid up in heaven beforehand, and not be left to be sent after (Matt. 6:20–21). And he who will make friends of the mammon of unrighteousness must now be rich toward God (Luke 12:21). It is no victory over the world to leave it when you cannot keep it. Nor will any legacy purchase heaven for an unholy, worldly soul.

The Faithful Stewardship of Estates

Yet they who will do good neither living nor dying are worst of all. Surely the last acts of our lives, if possible, should be the best. And as we must live in health, so also in sickness, and to the last in doing all the good we can. And, therefore, it must needs be a great sin to leave our estates to those who are like to do hurt with them, or to do no good, so far as we are the free disposers of them.

The case, I confess, is not without considerable difficulties, how much a man is bound to leave to his children or his nearest kindred, when some of them are disposed to live unprofitably, and some to live ungodlily and hurtfully. Some think men are bound to leave them nothing; some think they ought to leave them almost all; and some think that they should leave them only so much as may find them tolerable food and raiment. I shall do my best to decide the case in several propositions.

1. The case is not with us as it was with the Israelites, who might not alienate their inheritances from the tribes. Yet even they had power to prefer a younger son who was more deserving before an elder who was worse.

2. Where either law or contract has disabled a man to alienate his estate from an ungodly heir, there is no room for a doubt what he must do.

3. Nature teaches all men to prefer a child who is pious and hopeful in his provisions and legacies before a stranger who is somewhat better, and not to alienate his estate for want of a higher degree of goodness.

4. When there is a just cause to disinherit an elder son, a younger is to be preferred before a stranger, or a kinsman if there be no tolerable son.

5. And a son who ought not be trusted with riches or a great estate, yet ought to have food and raiment (unless he come to that state of obstinate rebellion in sin, for which God's law commanded the Israelites to bring forth their sons to be put to death. In such cases the house of correction is fittest for them). Yet he should have such food as may humble him, and not to gratify his lust.

6. If a man who has the full power to dispose of his estate, real or personal, has sons and kindred who, according to the judgment of sound reason, are likely if they had his estate to do mischief with it, or maintain them in a wicked life, or in a mere unprofitable life of idleness, living only to themselves and fleshly ease and pleasure, that man ought to give his estate from such to some who are more likely to do good with it, and to use it for God and the public benefit.

This is much contrary to the common course of most, who think no estate too great for their heirs nor any portion too great for their daughters, be they what they will or whatsoever use they are like to make of it. But these following reasons prove it to be true.

1. Every man has his estate from God, and for God, and is bound as his steward accordingly to use it. This is past doubt. And how does that man use it for God, who leaves it to one who is more likely to use it for the devil in a fleshly, unprofitable life? What account can such a steward give? Did God give it you to maintain idleness and sin?

   Objection. O but it is a son whom I am bound to provide for.

   Answer. Are you more bound to your son than to yourself? God does not allow you to spend it on yourself to maintain idleness and vice (Rom. 13:13–14): "Make no provision for the flesh, to fulfill its lusts (or will)." And may you leave it for such a use as is forbidden both your son and you? It is God who is the owner of it, and it is to him that you must both use and leave it: "Therefore, whether you eat or drink, or whatever you do, do it all to the glory of God" [1 Cor. 10:31]. And will you leave it to be the fuel of lust and sin?

   Obj. I leave it not for sin. But if he misuse it, I cannot help it.

   Ans. Would that excuse you if you put a sword into a madman's hand, to say, "I cannot help it if he use it ill?" You might have helped it. It is supposed that you foreknew how he was like to use it.

Obj. But he may prove better hereafter, as some do.

Ans. It is not bare possibilities that must guide a wise man's actions when probability is against them. Would you commit your children to the care of a madman or a knave because he may possibly come to his wits or become honest? Have you not long tried him, and have you not endeavored to cure him of his idleness, wickedness, or lust? If it be not done, what ground have you to presume it will be done when you are dead? You may have so much hope as not utterly to despair of him. But that will not allow you to trust him with that which God made you steward of, for his use and service.

But if such hopes may be gratified, give your estate in trust to some conscionable friend, with secret order to give it your son or kinsman if he becomes hereafter fit to use it according to the ends for which God gives it.

2. The obligation in my text of doing good to all extends to the end of our lives, and therefore to our last will and testament. Therefore, you must make your wills so as may do good to all, and not to cherish sin and idleness.

3. You are bound to your best to destroy sin and idleness and therefore not to feed and cherish it.

4. Doing good is the very thing that you are created, redeemed, and sanctified for, and therefore you must extend your endeavors to the

uttermost and to the last, that as much as may be, may be done when you are dead. If magistrates and ministers took care for no longer than their own lives, what would become of the state or church?

5. The common good is better than the plenty of a sinful child. Yes, it is to be preferred before the best child, and before ourselves, and therefore much more before the worst.

6. It is a dreadful thing to be guilty of all the fleshly sins that your ungodly sons will commit with your estate, when they shall by it maintain the sins of Sodom, pride, fullness of bread, and abundance of idleness, if not to strengthen their hands for oppression or persecution. To think that they will spend their days in voluptuousness because you gave them provision for the flesh!

7. It is cruelty to those who are already so bad to make their temptations to sin much stronger, and their place in hell the worse, and to make the way to heaven as hard to them as for a camel to go through the eye of a needle, to prepare them to want a drop of water in hell who were clothed richly and fared sumptuously on earth. It is cruelty to entice them to say, "Soul, you have many goods laid up for many years; take your ease; eat, drink, and be merry," until they hear, "Fool! This night your soul will be required of you" [Luke 12:19–20], to cherish that "friendship with the world is enmity with God" [James 4:4] by feeding that

lust of the flesh, and lust of the eyes, and pride of life, which are not of the Father but of the world [1 John 2:16].

8. When this preferring unprofitable and ungodly children before God and the common good is so common and reigning a sin in the world, it is a great fault for religious men to encourage them in it by their example and to do as they.

9. It is a sin to cast away any of God's gifts. When Christ had fed men by a miracle, he said, "Gather up the fragments that remain, so that nothing is lost" [John 6:12]. If you should cast your money into the sea, it would be a crime. But to leave it to such as you foresee are most likely to use it sinfully is more than casting it away.

   If you saw men offer sacrifice to Bacchus or Venus, you would abhor it. Do not that which is so like it, as to leave bad men fuel for fleshly lust.

10. It is the more dreadful, because it is dying in studied sin without repentance. To put so much sin into one's will shows a full consent and leaves no room and time to repent of it.

On all these accounts I advise all the stewards of God, as they love him and the public good and their own souls, while they have opportunity, even to the last breath, to do good to all, and to provide more for the common good than for superfluities to any and than for the maintaining ungodly children in sin, to the increase of their guilt and misery.

Indeed, in the choice of a calling, employment, and condition of life and place for their children, doing good should be preferred before their rising in the world. And they that justly endeavor to raise their families in wealth, honor, or power should do it only that they might do the more good. But it is Satan's design to turn all God's mercies to the cherishing of wickedness, and even the love of parents to their children to the poisoning of their souls, the strengthening of their snares, and the hindrance of their own and other men's salvation. But it is shame and pity, that they who in baptism devoted their children to God the Father, Son, and Holy Ghost, renouncing the world, the flesh, and the devil as under the banner of the cross, should labor all their life, that impenitently at death they may leave all that they can get to such as in all probability will use it in pride, fullness, and idleness for the flesh, the world, and the devil, against him and his interest from whom they received it, and to whom both they and all they had were once devoted.

When men are loath that their estates should remove from the name and family (for which there may be just cause) I take it for the safest way (as aforesaid) to trust some (as men do their children with guardians) by the advice of lawyers, to secure all from their unworthy heirs, for the next or some other of the name and lineage that proves worthy.

There are many other good works by which some rich men may be very profitable to the commonwealth, such as setting all the poor on work, and building hospitals for the impotent, and the like. But these this city is happily acquainted with already, and though still there be much wanting, yet there is much done.

An Additional Corollary for Merchants

But one more I will presume to name only to you that are merchants (for I am not one who has the ear of princes who are more able), might not somewhat more be done than yet is, to further the gospel in your factories and in our plantations? Old Mr. Eliot with his helpers in New England have shown that somewhat may be done, if others were as charitable and zealous as they.[1] The Jesuits and friars showed us in Congo, Japan, China, and other countries that much might be done with care and diligence. Though the papal interest was a corrupt end, and all the means that they used was not justifiable, when I read of their hazards, unwearied labors, and success, I am none of those that would deprive them of their deserved honor, but rather wish that we that have better ends and principles might do better than they, and not come so far behind them as we do (if half be true that Peter Maffaeus, and the Jesuits' epistles and many other writers tell us of them).[2] I know that they had the advantage of greater helps from kings and pope and prelates, and colleges endowed with trained men and copious maintenance. But might not somewhat more be done by us than is yet done?

---

1. John Eliot (c. 1604–1690), a Puritan missionary in New England, known as "the apostle to the Indians."

2. Giovanni Pietro Maffei, S.J. (1533–1603), known in English as John Peter Maffei or Maffaeus, was a Jesuit chronicler whose works include *Rerum a Societate Jesu in Oriente gestarvm tractatus* (Cologne: Calenium, 1573).

1. Is it not possible to send some able zealous chaplains to those factories which are in the countries of infidels and heathens? Such as thirst for the conversion of sinners and the enlargement of the church of Christ, and would labor skillfully and diligently therein? Is it not possible to get some short Christian books, which are fitted for that use, to be translated in such languages that infidels can read, and to distribute them among them? If it is not possible also to send thither religious, conscionable representatives who would further the work, the case of London is very sad.

2. Is it not possible, at least to help the poor, ignorant Armenians, Greeks, Russians, and other Christians who have no printing among them, nor much preaching or knowledge, and for want of printing have very few Bibles, even for their churches or ministers? Could nothing be done to get some Bibles, catechisms, and practical books printed in their own tongues and given among them? I know there is difficulty in the way. But money and willingness and diligence might do something.

3. Might not something be done in other plantations as well as in New England towards the conversion of the natives there? Might not some skillful, zealous preachers be sent thither, who would both promote serious piety among those of the English that have too little of it and might invite the Americans to learn the gospel, and teach our planters how to behave themselves Christianly toward them, to win them to Christ?

4. Is it not possible to do more than has been done to convert the blacks who are our own slaves or servants to the Christian faith? Has not Mr. Goodwin justly reprehended and lamented the neglect, yes, and resistance of this work in Barbados, and the like elsewhere?[3]

a. Might not better teachers be sent thither for that use?

b. Is it not an odious crime for Christians to hinder the conversion of these infidels, lest they lose their service by it, and to prefer their gain before men's souls? Is not this to sell souls for a little money, as Judas did his Lord? And whereas the law manumits them from servitude when they turn Christians that it may invite them to conversion, and this occasions wicked Christians to hinder them from knowledge, were it not better to move the government therefore to change that law, so far as to allow these covetous masters their service for a certain time, using them as free servants?

c. And whereas they are allowed only the Lord's Day for their own labor, and some honest Christians would willingly allow them some other time instead of it that they might spend the Lord's Day in learning to know Christ and worship God, but they dare not do it, lest their wicked

---

3. Morgan Godwyn (fl. 1685) was an Anglican clergyman and fierce advocate for the spiritual welfare of slaves.

neighbors rise against them for giving their slaves such an example, might not the governors be procured to force the whole plantation to it by a law, even to allow their infidel servants so much time on another day, and cause some to congregate them for instruction on the Lord's Days? Why should those men be called Christians, or have any Christian reputation or privileges themselves, who think both Christianity and souls to be no more worth than to be thus basely sold for the gain of men's most servile labors? And what, though the poor infidels desire not their own conversion, their need is the greater, and not the less.

Conclusion

I conclude with this moving inference: the great opposition that is made against doing good by the devil and his whole army through all the world, and their lamentable success, does call aloud to all true Christians to overdo them. O what a kingdom of evildoers has Satan doing mischief to men's souls and bodies through the earth! Hating the godly; oppressing the just; corrupting doctrine; introducing lies; turning Christ's laborers out of his vineyard; forbidding them to preach in his name the saving word of life; hiding or despising the laws of Christ and setting up their own wills and devices in their stead; making dividing, distracting engines on pretense of order, government, and unity; murdering men's bodies, and ruining their estates, and slandering their names on pretense of love to the church and souls; encouraging profaneness, blasphemy, perjury, whoredom, and scorning conscience and fear of sinning. What diligence does Satan use through the very Christian nations to turn Christ's ordinances of magistracy and ministry against himself, and to make his own officers the most mischievous enemies to his truth and kingdom and saving work? To tread down his family and spiritual worship, as if it were by his own authority and commission? To preach down truth, and conscience, and real godliness, as in Christ's own name, and fight against him with his own word and to teach the people to hate his servants, as if this pleased the God of love?

And alas! How dismal is their success? In the East the church is hereby destroyed by barbarous Muslims. The remnants by their prelates continued in sects, in great ignorance and dead formality, reproaching and anathematizing one another, and little hope appearing of recovery. In the West a dead image of religion and unity and order, dressed up with a multitude of gods and set up against the life and soul of religion, unity, and order, and a war hereupon maintained for their destruction, with sad success. So that usually the more zealous men are for the papal and formal human image, the more zealously they study the extirpation of worshiping God in spirit and truth, and thirst after the blood of the most serious worshipers, and cry down them as intolerable enemies, who take their baptism for an obliging vow and seriously endeavor to perform it and live in good earnest as Christianity binds them. And they take it for an insufferable crime to prefer God's authority before man's, and to plead his law against anything that men command them. In a word, he is unworthy to be accounted a Christian with them who will be a Christian indeed and not despise the laws of Christ, and unworthy to have the liberty and usage of a man who will not sin and damn his soul. So much more cruel are they than the Turkish tyrants who, if they send to a man for his head, must be obeyed.

And is the devil a better master than Christ? And shall his work be done with greater zeal and resolution? Will he give his servants a better reward? Should not all this awaken us to do good with greater diligence than they do evil? And to promote love and piety more earnestly than they do malignity and iniquity? Is not saving church and state, souls and bodies, better worth resolution and labor than destroying them?

And the portents are encouraging. Certainly Christ and his kingdom will prevail. At last all his enemies shall be made his footstool, yes, shall from him receive their doom, to the everlasting punishment that rebels against omnipotence, goodness, and mercy do deserve. If God be not God, if Christ will not conquer, if there be no life to come, let them boast of their success. But when they are rottenness and dust, and their souls with devils, and their names are a reproach, Christ will be Christ, his promises and threats all made good. He will judge it righteous to recompense tribulation to your troublers when he comes with his mighty angels in flaming fire to take vengeance on rebels, and to be glorified in his saints, and admired in all true believers (2 Thess. 1:6–10). And when that solemn judgment shall pass on those who did good, and who did evil (described in Matthew 25 with a "Come, you blessed of My Father, inherit the kingdom," and "Depart from Me, you cursed, into the everlasting fire"), doing good and not doing it (much more doing mischief) will be better distinguished than now they are, when they are rendered as the reason of those different dooms.

Scripture Index

OLD TESTAMENT

NEW TESTAMENT